THIS
FAR
FROM THE
SOURCE

ALSO BY NEIL SHEPARD

Scavenging the Country for a Heartbeat

I'm Here Because I Lost My Way

Neil Shepard

POEMS

THIS
FAR
FROM THE
SOURCE

MID-LIST PRESS
Minneapolis

Published by Mid-List Press
4324 12th Avenue South, Minneapolis, MN 55407-3218
Visit our website at www.midlist.org.

Library of Congress Cataloging-in-Publication Data
Shepard, Neil, 1951-
  This far from the source : poems / Neil Shepard.
     p. cm.
  ISBN-13: 978-0-922811-72-4 (trade paper ed. : alk. paper)
  ISBN-10: 0-922811-72-5 (trade paper ed. : alk. paper)
  I. Title.
  PS3569.H39395T57 2006
  811'.54—dc22
                                    2006019871

Manufactured in the United States of America
First printing: September 2006

Cover photo: "Minnesota River, Mendota" by Mark A. Kawell.
Copyright © 2006 by Mark A. Kawell

Text and cover design: Lane Stiles

CONTENTS

ONE

WATERFALL AT

JOURNEY'S

END

Yet another metamorphic
swimming hole, waterfall
where language fails.

Gneiss, schist, slate.
You can hear nouns meta-
morphose to verbs, *gnarl, shiver, split,*

then strip down, tumble
in granitic kettle-holes
and camouflage themselves

in green water, green
because pines hang
above the fault line

and shade language
from blue-blank sky where some-
body's watching, listening

to the syllables of delight.
This is the place of pre-
delight, before the light

blinked on in our fore-
brains and pained us with fore-
knowing. No, this place

delivers a hiss, a wordless
rush through gray clefts,
the high chattering scream

of being submerged in momentary
cold so cold the body knows
undeniably, indelibly,

these are the high walls
of journey's end, of anaerobic
last-gasp, body-turning

blue. And tongues become
like limbs trying to climb
the high cliffs of death

to clutch a purchase
on exposed outcrops
where words can sink

their cleats, pitons,
grappling hooks, inventions
that turn humans pre-

human: moss-crawler, rock-clasper,
some thing attached to cold stone
that owns no language—

micaceous, gneiss-spark,
fissile schist, granite-fault—
that goes on climbing

as if it were stone-dumb,
attached by its tongue
to the thing, the very thing.

how the box turtle crosses
the road, or doesn't, its shell crushed

by a produce truck, or not, and the eggs
are spawned in a sandy ditch, perhaps

where the turtle ranks deposited
for generations their inheritance.

In order to see as I see,
Homer's hexameter had to turn

Odysseus homeward, wandering
across the Aegean, and consciousness

turn ever inward, Descartes' *ergo sum*
centrifuge out the self, suspended,

from the element of otherness,
and Darwin's *Beagle* bump up

against a being from Galapagos,
whose ancient hooded eyes

were so much not our own
that Rousseau wept and painted

scenes of savage greenery,
while science praised the progress

of our opposable thumb,
its blueprints and hammered nails,

and humans felt afresh the home
they'd lost, the one they'd carried

on their backs, wherever they wandered,
always, everywhere, at home.

Tea–cher, tea–cher, tea–cher, teach
me something I don't already know.
Oh ovenbird, come out of the shade
and cook up a reason for the shad's
spring petals showering the forest
with soft release: *Optima dies
prima fugit.* **We–see, we–see, we–see**
all the hungers: in black-and-white
warbler's beak stuffed with neon-green
worms, honeysuckle's spindly flowers
alive with black-and-yellow bees,
blue moths tumbling from apple blossoms.
Watch those who harvest fiddleheads,
who wield the greedy hands of spring,
lop off the gold-green stems, then swat
at midges and shadflies. Complain,
they must, about the body's status
as blood-dinner for lusty insects,
buzzing ciphers who'd sting and suck
us dry simply because it's encoded
in their cryptograms, but death
requires us as the honored hosts
of endless last suppers. Mystery's
when we turn the other cheek
and offer it, when we become
more than the body's surviving
codes. Unleash the hungers
beneath the hunger, the dragon-
fly all morning alight on granite
ledge, beside a multitude of bugs,
untouched, simply because sun on stone
feels so near the source, so atavistic,
even a darning needle's pricked awake.

Even a human on the run must
pause in a field of blue forget-me-not.
Even that swiftest of self-preser-
vationists, Atalanta, stopped
and stooped for three luscious, golden
apples, even if it meant self-
desecration, surrender to
the thing that would devour her.

Notes:
1. Bolded phrases are birdcalls of the ovenbird and black-and-white warbler, as interpreted by Peterson's *A Field Guide to Birds East of the Rockies*.
2. *Optima dies prima fugit*: "The best day is the first to flee" (a line from the Roman poet Virgil).

(Sweetbriar, Virginia)

I'm old enough to know this daylight
savings time's a ruse, yet I'm out here
near sundown, haunting one more hour
of light, inhaling flowers like there's no
tomorrow: lilacs, especially lilacs,
that incarnate bait: open your mouth,
waft this in, now tell me you don't want a body.
And there's more where that came from: bleeding
heart, marsh marigold, blossom of plum and persimmon,
all floating in spring ether. I'm out here, suckered
by spring and this heart—what to do but smother it
in flowers, daylight savings flowers that come
long before the first gold hues of leaves,
longer still before inexorable green
spoils my mood. Green says I'm growing
old and mute as moss. In April rain, May
swell, June fulcrum, July slide, August dust,
I hear it. And September, September's leaves
hang like dog-eared pages I'd rather not read
again. Oh, for October where together we tear
to shreds those stories of second comings, watch
them fall down around us. The older I grow,
the closer in age to god, who is timeless.
Soon I'll be going home. Today, I'm burying my face
in flowers, trying to smell from the living side
what it'll be like when I'm swimming
in flowers, and I don't smell a thing.

Something about sultry Virginia,
the way a woodpecker drilling a hollow bole
sends a dew-heavy *sugar-plum*, a love tap,
echoing across the distance. Morning air's
heavy, scented, capable of carrying
a sound longer than its source,
the dulcimer hammer of the woodpecker
still echoing in my ear. Something about
a western wind, a meadowlark's spiralling
call that puts me in the mind of high
romanticism, out of favor, for sure,
but woefully misunderstood as fashion.
No, it's a *mood* inside us, *always*, that responds:
Virginia's time-exalted and ample atmosphere.
Or what science might describe as ionized air,
particles inducing melancholy or joy,
depending on prevailing winds, wind-
speed, and salt levels in the brain.
Or what the shrink in his office
tapping his watch to say the hour's up—
like a drag on timelessness—
might describe as my ego's
manic phase. (Yes, and more somber
moods abound, guided by the classical
aridity of Arizona or the depressed ironies
of Northeastern cities.) Listen to me.
My echo. Far from its hollow
source. It was such a pleasant morning.
The mood was *sugar-plum*, and I was leaning
over purple clusters of forget-me-not, dreaming
they were still true and beautiful.

I'm ready to murder the flowers.
The allnight wordfest, verbal *festschrift*—
which, notice, I do not hyphenate
because Coleridge warns us against
invented compounds bound by hyphens—
left me in some indeterminate schwa
of sleeplessness, neither long on yawns
nor persnickety and testy,
but stunned, stoned, seemingly
systematically taken apart
by human sounds—verbs, nouns, the little
modifiers, expletives, pronominals,
signs and referents, all, all part of
human grammar (that thing I love)
and "human drama" (that thing I hate)
which kept me listening, listening
for their rhetorical flourishes—
lean in for the sweet *soto voce*,
then gradually lean out for the rising
tonal babel, snickers, snorts,
giggles and guffaws, interrogatory,
exclamatory, imperative, imperious,
ablative, declarative, hortatory,
denunciatory, importuning, simpering,
sniveling, wheedling, whining, oh!—
it kept me up all night, allnight long
while the flowers closed their ears
and slept. I'll murder them! I will!

THE IMMORTAL

The mountains are old,
but I am older
and claim no immortal soul.
Iron and *mica* are old words,
strong and glinting,
but *dust* is older still
and has a harrowing brilliance.

When I awoke God
was in my head. For centuries
He spoke to me. Then I slept
the sleep of mountains and rivers,
and woke to know him a dream I'd made
many times, one less substantial
than the sand in my eyes.

I was older than he
and would live forever
in the labors of the universe,
a woman's birth, or a star's,
and would live in the dust,
indistinguishable from the least
particle of light, unextinguished.

A thousand feet down, the Rio Grande daily
reinscribes itself on scrolls of sandstone.
Look down, and there's a recondite text revealed:
earth history that snakes like uro-
boros; beneath it another creature
reified from the obscure. There's a millennium
instarred in mud, times of plague and pestilence.
And a signature of solfatura,
a few lines of blasphemy. There's a comet's
pink penmanship and the blue formation
of heavens, and a black scrawl of beginnings.
And close to the surface the condign
mea culpas of slow-witted creatures
who have just learned to think and are still
wet with rising from the waters, still
crossing over on the first day,
though they believe they have come so far.

TWO

SICK DAY

SICK DAY

In the beginning
I lie and feel the lie is good.
I call in sick, then kick in bed,
a free man. I watch an hour of snow
beyond the picture window, then watch
a TV show. Bolsheviks are changing

the world again. Laura and Zhivago
slip away to an ice palace, their love
smoldering and licking frost from the panes
until the cold moon comes
through a small circle of flesh-
warmed glass. Upon my knees,

I place the Rolodex and flip
through the usual love interests
(Susan and Susanne and Suzanne).
Then I make myself look at the old
marriage albums. I make myself.

Then the film unravels in real time,
Zhivago up late, staring into the candle's
separations: red flame at the wick, bud
of passion; yellow flame one remove
from the source; blue flame at the fringe,
become impersonal as Arctic sky.

Red encased in yellow, like a tiny hook
and hammer, feverish, struggling,
on a plain of yellowing passion.
Zhivago, up late listening, listening
to language tangling with the cries of wolves
starving on the tundra. I surf away,

channel-flip a hundred years to news
of corporate czars, merging, pledging
profits for the greater good—
downsizing, restructuring, flattening
wages. Working stiffs are stiffed again.

Surf back, and Sharif's fabulous
eyes are sad, his doctor's bag
packed, prepared to minister
to the greater good. In all that snow
outside his window and outside mine,
what is this greater thing? How is it

best ministered to? In flickering images
of history—like candle flames opening holes
in window ice—we see our human fates.
We know how Bolsheviks rose and fell.
We know how love extinguished for the greater
good gives both the truth and lie to *agape*.

Now cut to the chase. Moscow.
Zhivago old, hunched, trudging
down an imperially icy street.
Oh shut it off, shut it off. I know
the rest. Laura's disheveled hair.
Zhivago's heart broken in the street.
Give us some air, please!

Oh, this sick day grows sicker
and the lie goes sour. With one free
hour, I feel the weight of what's missing.
Without her, the world's heavier.
It's red with fever, hunger.
I'll pack my black bag and go out.

OIL TRUST

We've come to Gaines County where Great-Uncle Ned
once figured the fortune beneath the soil,
then nailed it down. Now, he owns the blackness
beneath the earth. He invested his life in it—
drill, pump, girder—then the long years came due.
He's been down there ever since, but his silver
derricks still intersect the sky,

pumping up black pools, converting them
to cash, and I like to think
a little of him has been converted, too,
from flesh and bone to earth again,
and, who knows, in a million years,
if he and his fellow occupants of time
and common dust won't pool their talents

into oil again. Odder conversions
have happened: his kin turned
lefty pink, leaked profits by the barrelful
to grassroots groups against Big Oil.
They broke his trust, but still the oil
kept coming, and keeps coming. It's our turn,
now. We're here to make our claim.
The surface soil's still good and red.

Sharecroppers work it for peanuts and cotton.
We watch them hack and hoe, then turn toward Brown
& Brown, to sign a few forms, claim our share
of the crude. Afterward, we bury ourselves
far from the sun, in the county's
only espresso bar, its clientele squeezed
between saddle shops, granaries, and a few
dusty bars. We're from elsewhere, sure as shit.

South of town, twisters kick up red dust
and bring it in—it settles on everything:
on cash-crop pecans and measly greasewood;
on sharecropper shacks in the shadow
of Wal-Mart; on migrant tents beside the faux-
Spanish villas; on crude oil pumps; on all of us.
Powdered like this, we look prematurely wise.

By dusk, we make our way to Tru-Value Inn,
a neon lariat against the sky.
In the parking lot, a few cowboys
drag on cigarettes and let their wide vowels
drift off; a few migrant workers
lean against farm trucks and tip back beers.
We all pause when flashing lights and sirens pass.

This evening's an opening I recognize—
life's circumstances reduced, or enlarged,
to big sky, stunted trees, and mesas
bridging the land all the way to Mexico.
Tonight, the grander design
might reveal itself: the revolutions
of an ambulance light; a circling

lariat; oil pumps drawing up the dead
matter of millennia and converting it
to gold. How much can we give away
and still frequent the espresso bar?
Whose faces are these in the polished chrome
of coffee urns and spangled mirrors?
Whose faces are these mesmerized
by the red dust still settling on the lot of us?

Predawn behind a cloudbank, Rockies gray.
I walk past Motel 6 and out of town. Thirty years ago,
these plains were wind and sagebrush, diamondback and washout.
Now Hewlett-Packard, UPS and Western Bell corral the land;
high-tension wires surround high-walled cinderblock.
The clouds descend from peaks, down hogbacks bristling

resistance before rain falls uniformly on the plains.
I wander past warehouses where sunflowers loop the barbed wire,
loll gray-green in predawn. Two ragged figures,
guzzling wine, loaf on a trash heap
beside a dead-end railroad line
where boxcar doors are open, half-loaded

with the latest gimmickry. Allen? Jack?
They're drunk and not with poetry.
They're reading invoices, not "in voices,"
reciting the math by which men die daily:
666 machines, 66 megabytes of memory . . .
They're drunk but dutiful. And now a sunrise wind

rips papers from their hands. The ragged figures
scramble after them like stumbling monkeys . . .
Back, back past Rent-A-Wreck and villages
of U-Store-It, past sunflowers, dropping
seeds by the road side, ready to grow
anywhere. O Sunflower, you're too eager

to sow holiness in every wayside heap.
The night clerk I left snoring is sober-gray.
The yawning maids await the day's stained
sheets, stare into filmy coffee. In this high country,
clouds dissolve in tracts of sun. Gray dawn's forgotten.
Heavy machinery busts sod for another lot, and billboards

hail the clean air here. Though sun rises and lights up
the Mummy Range, I feel this cloudbank
still upon the world and cannot see my way,
though sunflowers wave their brilliant heads
as if the world had found its soul again
and phantoms once more solidified as men.

When I moved to Baton Rouge,
last refuge of the Fugitives,
the university writers proffered Southern
hospitality in mock-heroic fashion.
There were mighty allusions to the barbarians
at the gates, as they inclined their noses
toward shanty town, toward the iron bars
on their windows masquerading as black grille.
And our host, a big-wig writer, showed us
a Kentucky Derby baseball bat, painted red,
my Red Stick, he said, to keep the hordes
at bay, to bash a few black fingers
if they pick my locks or "unscrew my doorjambs."
Their looks went blank, then black
when I mentioned the politics of prosody—
free verse's egalitarian sprawl versus
formal verse's upper-class refinement,
how Robert Lowell's loosening lines and rhymes
led from patrician Boston to "doing time,"
to C.O. status, "For the Union Dead," and
Colonel Shaw's "angry wren-like vigilance"—
and they steered me back to an earlier tale
of Lowell decamping patrician Boston
to camp on Tate's Southern lawns
and learn from the Master.
As they toasted to the last Agrarians,
I raised my glass of Old Kentucky
and watched a cockroach float down
from the high ceiling to squirt inside
my shirt. Those Southern writers
hadn't seen a thing until I screamed,
burst a few buttons, and released
the Kafkaesque roach from my chest.

From there, in a matter of hours,
my Southern hosts remembered
a vacant apartment I could rent.
They set me up in an all-black block
of shotgun shacks upgraded, by a front stoop
and back storage shed, to city code.
And I might have lived happily
if I hadn't been white.
I might have loved Tabby's Blues Bar,
just around the corner, with its jangling
guitars and crackling PA whenever
the singer threatened to "drink muddy water,
sleep in a hollow log." But the black bartender
wouldn't serve me. I refused to read
the black rage in his eyes until he
and three others sat down at my table:
"Get your white ass gone, if you want to keep it."
Yes, I might have lived happily
if my tires weren't slashed each week,
my place ransacked, the walls spray-painted:
GET YOUR WHITE ASS GONE!
I moved out, moved farther south
of town where the Fugitives lived
behind their suburban grilles.
The big-wig offered his Red Stick:
"I've got a dozen in my closet."
Though I refused it, I wanted it. I wanted it.
And I hated it perhaps even more than
you do, reading this, thinking, his choice
is as easy as black and white. Well,
what would you choose? The red stick
or the bloody handshake? The black
grille-work or the white-ass

pound of flesh paid back? For a while,
I stored up my stories, sharpened my irony,
and waited for the next Northern boy to arrive
with his social-class critique. At the time,
I didn't know how deeply progressive
fear is, how thin the surface of kindness,
how radically the best go on turning
the other cheek. Colonel Shaw turning
his back on his fuming, shamefaced father
and leading his black troops southward
to civil war, Lowell pulling up stakes
on the Master's Southern lawn, tuning his verse
to the rhythm of civil rights, and turning
back to Boston, to protest and jail time, to the radical
disruptions of a free verse line that would lead
him closer to Colonel Shaw's marching men.

CORFU

Late afternoon we watch the waters change—
aquamarine, cerulean, royal blue, blue-violet.
And now, violet, deep violet. And now black.

The patio lights say your eyes are blue, your lids
purple, your skin copper. The glow of Greek morning's
still upon your face. And what came later—

something far from the jeweled coastlines
and secret coves where lovers dive, make love,
preserve each others' bodies with sun oils.

Somewhere far into the interior of the island
where groves of orange, lemon, lime, shiver
in heat, where fragrant myrrh and olive

mask a far older smell. All comes back to us
this evening in the sweep of mountain wind.
We feel a certain nakedness remembering

the backfire of our mopeds on the mountain
road, young fruit-pickers perched in the foliage,
their heads emerging like globed fruits as we passed.

Arriving in a whitewashed village,
we blew black smoke in siesta-sun,
until the children pegged pebbles, pointing

and running and begging. Women's black-veiled heads hung
out their windows, and their bony fingers pointed.
Town-fathers plied us with *ouzo, retsina,*

then wrapped their legs around us in an old
Ionian dance, and their hunger drove us
farther out on the mountain road where blind

beggar-widows huddle in their black shawls.
As we sputtered and belched black fumes, they caught us
in the cross hairs of their eyeless stares, worse than

the eye of the all-knowing, two black holes for sockets,
and the leprous nose, and that last hole
of darkness where the mouth opens in need,

the language foreign but familiar to any traveler.
Tonight we still see them as the Corfu waters
go violet, go black. Hands rise from scaly limbs

and they beg with their missing fingers.

Because Morton Sobel would not, would not sing,
not fink, not rat, on his friends, and took the fifth,
and used amendments better men had made to presume
his innocence, and chose silence's accurate no-account,
to sound's waffling testimony . . .

GERALD STERN SANG

last night on the phone to me,
"Sixteen Minutes" from his early book *Odd Mercy,*
because somewhere in those many sections lies
one reference to my lovely Irish wife's step-
father, Morton Sobel, now far removed from that sorry
chapter of American history and infamy
he shares with his friends Ethel and Julius
Rosenberg, long dead now, long shot
with a killing voltage, while Morty survived
30 years in federal pens, Alcatraz, until it closed,
and later, Lewisburg, where across town from the pen,
young Jerry Stern was tunneling out of the prison
of another poem, into a lighter, risible space,
this time, a long one about the vast cells and sentences
of history, the land masses locked in their hatreds,
but in his mind, they could float together like clouds,
integrate, to form one peaceable "Judish Irishaloyem,"
and the Sobel reference seemed accountably cautious,
as if Stern, his own family half-Jewish, half-Irish,
half-subversive, half-fearful of "the monster Siberia
with Alaska in its mouth," couldn't choose between allegiances,
or maybe, in that swirl of half-truths and Red-scare called the 50s,
that shredding of evidence in the confetti of another election year,
couldn't ferret out the guilt or innocence, and so hugged
to the historical record—"Sobel/who spent twenty years
here because he kept his bomb/in a cardboard suitcase
underneath a girder/on the Williamsburg Bridge"—

and gave Sobel not a word of his own. Morty, who lived
the middle of his life in a solitary cell, sometimes deprived
of pen and paper, deprived of any human voice but his own,
but went on speaking and writing the book
in his head, *On Doing Time*, for 18 years,
until, looking back and looking back, he was turned
by time into an ossified artifact, and history
removed the human sting of those passions,
and he was deemed safe as a wasp preserved in amber.
Finally, the many hands of government set time going
again for this man, and the iron door clanged open,
and he left with his one set of clothes and scraps
of paper and words in his head that would become his one book—
and young Jerry Stern, at Bucknell for one semester, to write one
of many books, a man with words bursting from his chest,
could not *not* write about it, although he could barely
read the waffling testimonies that passed for history,
knew only and vaguely that all our rights trembled
and shimmered on the Lewisburg prison walls, unless
the human voice floated out to unsay the sentences
that have said men wrongly into history and infamy,
and so, as poets do, out of the moment's
half-truth, lyrical impulse, shape-shifting capacity, self-
appointment with arrogance and shadow, and what passes
for beauty, he wrote "Sixteen Minutes" for men out of time,
and brought them into time, and tonight, after time
has rendered Stern's verse inconsequential as factual record,
it comes to me as singing, long passages of it
lilting, long-distance over the phone, Jerry Stern,
whom I hardly know, and on my nickel, grabs his book
off the shelf and reads and reads, as if the one true
conversation were this, valueless, as the meter
keeps ticking, valueless, as the voice transmits,

across whatever distance, its rendering of how time
flows through us and teaches us our ignorance,
and how what we say imprisons us, then releases us
to say the next thing, and the next, dispensing
blue elegy or green cheer, gray veracity
or white doubt, as we go from disaster
to disaster, singing, without a doubt, singing.

THREE

I'M FROM
LEOMINSTER,
COULDN'T BE PROUDER

At 80, father seems to live forever,
body still hale and well muscled
on a chaise longue, but his mind's loose
and flapping in a ragged place
he calls "the mind's dumpster," scavenging
the same memories six times an hour . . .
like those clips of Maine coast summers
he used to film, splicings of family
faces squinting into sun, grinning,
tossing kisses, years before they'd go
missing. And half a reel given over
entirely to gulls. Nothing more.
Close-ups and clips of squawking groups.
We'd laugh when family films spilled
onto these frames, yelled *Fast-forward!*
lest seagulls eclipse all our relations.
Over time, father laughed with us,
but that first time his eyes registered
displeasure. What had we missed?
He could not say, or would not.
Pleasure of feathered ones, so distant,
so distinct from us no bridge exists,
not even human mind, to bridge it?
What was it father knew? What love
drove him to film those gulls,
now long crashed in surf or sand, long turned
to other matter, as have our ancestors?
Clips of the eclipsed. Cells illumined
in celluloid. But what was his intention?
Just light, motion, observing eye—
in short, domain of birdbrain—
or something keener? To see
as birdbrain sees? Without the edge

of history—foreseen, foreknown—
trembling in late-day sun, clouding
all we see: father asleep on the chaise,
his full definition reduced to repeating
images on the screen of his mind.
What is the meaning of memory
this far from the source? It's summer,
always summer in father's Maine coast films.

Unlike today's stark shots: father,
midwinter, coast of Florida, sound
asleep among the snowbirds, seagulls
circling overhead, seagulls
circling down, seagulls perching
near the chaise, scavenging
whatever we've left them.

WHEEZE

Peewee's under the eaves,
its song wheezier than phoebe's—

both of them inside my head,
I think they use the same nest—

just as catbird and thrasher
are wheezier than mockingbird,

just as mother's wheezier
than sister, father more mocking

than his sons. It's hell
in full sunlight to see things

out of the shade. Glaring,
hurtful to the eyes. Asthmatic gasps

come from the bedrooms, first sister's,
then mother's, where father flies

between them. Little competitions,
border songs and nesting sites,

and who's to bed with whom.
I see it clearly now, lower the field

glasses, and listen. Listen hard.
Yes, he's singing, too. A mocking

song, to keep his sons from the breeding
ground. Flitting between two nests,

for all he's worth, flitting, mocking.
To keep us fledglings, always. Always.

I've been holding my breath
for sixty billion
nanoseconds.

One minute. Inspiring
my lungs to—what?—
release words. Then

the next, words inter-
rupted, ruptured, ex-
piring, as si-

lence shatters. That weed whacker.
That lawnboy, sweating
and bellowing

along to a rock song
on his Walkman, whacks
deep paths in weedy

memory. Is this
as it should be, noise
converted to

poetry? My past was
never a high tower,
leisure the be-

all and end-all of culture,
but a low-class house,
polluted town,

no bones about it, said
father, no pansy-
ass, limp-wristed

writers here. Mouths-to-feed
earn their keep, penny
a word. Count them

in nanoseconds, count
them while the lawn-
mower chokes and clogs

every word you ever had.
After chores, your head
was a hum, a-

buzz in bubblegum chat-
ter and AM tran-
sistor, nothing

like the muse's hushed cave,
where words trickled through
clefts in a skull.

In the fenced-in yard, in
the hot sun, he bel-
lows. And I do,

I still do count
in nanoseconds
all the lily-

livered words mowed down
by six buzzing kin
vying for air-

time at the table, time
in my head. They won't
stop talking, stop

whacking away at the silence.
Penny a word, write
wherever you are,

the lawn mower going,
TV on (always),
the canned sounds

of late-day (soap) opera,
culture of melodrama.
Write as you mow.

Now, whack the weeds.

Sun at apogee from earth.
I feel it, and don't feel it:
light's slight sting. Death,
where is *thy* sting?
It's out there. He's out there.
Father, father, I'm cold.
You're so far off. Your massive
gravity no longer holds.
Your animal magnetism.
Your ancient warmth.
I'm coming undone
from the old rotations
and will absolutely
spin off into cold space,
into unidentifiable dark—
if you don't come back soon.

Each year we wager
a few dust motes
against the ecliptic
and bank on your return.
Will this be the winter
you loose your bonds?
Don't go. I know how
this is wrong. I'm pre-
Copernican. The sun's
desertion is in my way
of seeing. Earth
orbits sun. Perhaps it's I
who longed to pull away,
aphelion, live as if
on the moon's dark side. Wait.
Who could have called
this sea "Tranquillity?"

TEENAGER: 13

A simple pimple
calls all its cousins
from an Italian Catholic clan
and parties on your face.
Now you're a pepperoni pizza—
grease, cheese, red sauce oozing
from your skin, mooning

over June Martin who's broken
your heart again, her rich fistfuls
of raven hair locked around a luckier
boy's fingers, her bright scarves
knotted precisely for him. You take
her notes and pass them to the one
she's freely chosen for free

ice-cream floats and banana boats.
Frozen sweets. Sweet delay
before the maraschino cherry's eaten.
Your heart's broken but will grow
back again, stronger, stranger,
like the Blob or the Thing or the diced
skeletons among the Argonauts—

like all monstrosities, willful
and hungry for all the toppings. Thirteen
and you're a pizza man: black olives, pepperoni,
mozzarella clogging your pores. On the other hand,
you skin's oiled, alive, desire swimming
over your face like schools of anchovies,
little silver tongues fresh from the Cote d'Azure.

This isn't funny, for you.
Suicides beyond the mirror
of the medicine chest, detonations
of self-regard, still bury
their blackheads in your cheeks.
I know there's light at the end
of the tunnel, even if it is ambulance-light,

disco-flashing, livening up a black
humorist's party. This comedy
is my salary, my tip,
as if I were the pizza man delivering,
in under 30 minutes, the one thing
to feed you before your hunger
consumes you. Meanwhile,

someone's suffering, changing
into a new hand that fits a new glove,
a new voice that fits a new register.
One day, you'll be like me:
deep-dish pizza, Greek
olives, Feta cheese, and artichoke
hearts, which, at the moment,

might as well be Greek to you—
subtle, slightly yellowed hearts,
almost laughable, hidden under folds
of spiny leaves and hairy
green I had no idea was there,
no idea how to undress
when I was thirteen.

What *was* a panty raid, anyway, I wondered,
as I sniffed the spring breeze, May 4th, 1970,
Burlington, Vermont, waiting for my roommate
to douse himself in Brute and Binaca?
Would we gather *our* cotton underwear in hands
that had known no harvest, parade across campus,
waving them like flags or clouds or dreams drifting
toward our future? Or was it *their* panties
we were after, to snatch from clotheslines, tumbling
dryers, open drawers, or that barely
imaginable triangle where radars jammed
and things went wildly off course? The stiff wind
held far-off towns and clouds gunmetal gray as dusk
closed over. When finally we were revved, bursting,
flashlights powering holes in the night sky,
ready to divvy up whatever loot we'd find—
when, in short, we were strapped in, ready for
the long ride to manhood, or wherever we thought we were going,
the leaders relayed the change in plans,
the radio news—that monks had wrapped
themselves in robes of flame, and soldiers wrapped
in body bags were flying home, and now this—
this rumor grown to legend and legend to life,
until we all tasted metal in our mouths and something else,
hot and desperate and large, undeniably among us that was
not us alone, and four names were on our tongues, four names
as we marched away from our teens and toward that strange country
called twenty, and as for me, a fifth name was on the wind
that night, a name marching toward me across the college green,
a vigil-candle cupped in her small hands, and whether
I got in her panties that night I cannot say, for the wind
was up and the rain came down and we cupped our candles
for all we were worth, trying to keep that guttering flame
going as long as we could for the four dead in Ohio.

I'M FROM LEOMINSTER, COULDN'T BE PROUDER, CAN'T HEAR ME NOW, I'LL YELL A LITTLE LOUDER

I can still hear it down the years:
the grand architecture of that cheer.

In megaphones, in unison, the fans
chanting with the cheerleaders, building, building

the round vowels—*prouder, louder* —and the
two-line rhyme itself endless until its pitch

raised the rafters. On so little we build
our pride. On mass conviction and massive

self-regard. On so little it crumbles.
Stub your toes on it awhile. Scuff that art-

ifact to a bruised shine. What pride was at stake
when public school destroyed parochial?

Our boastful jocks kicked ass. Religious boys
were sissies, short-breathed from prayers.

So Leominster nailed them to the cross
with a full-court press. Saint Joan's went down,

clutching their sides. Saint Bernard's littered
the floor with sprained ankles. What church did we build

from those victories? In history,
we learned Rome built *duomos* for its saints—

for one, Saint Catherine, to house her bones,
and still returned her skull to archrival

Siena so its patron saint could bask
in hometown cheers and prayers. We learned

Venetians led a Holy War to beat up Turks
and other infidels who lived across the tracks,

then stole Saint Mark from Alexandria,
filched Saint Lucy from Constantinople,

plucked up Saint Roch from his parents' chateau,
but built them cathedrals, yes, cathedrals

modeled on Egypt, Byzantium, and
France, respectfully. Compared to them,

we're brutes who glorify our towns with home-
town cheers and sneer at creeds or faith

from foreign places. What kids did you knock down
because they lived across the line? What dust-

offs, beanballs, did you toss at batters?
What blind-side blocks, illegal tackles?

Can't hear me now? I'll yell a little louder.
I've come for the day, praying I no longer

measure up to Leominster's hubristic
inches. This is my humbling devotional.

I'm eyeing my old home through waves of ghosts.
I'm superman reduced to just one power:

the power of pastness. My x-ray vision
sees through walls, sees the halls those kids

perpetually in need of rescue ran through:
brothers, sisters, mother, father, everyone

proud as punches in the chest, thumps and high-
fives for some conquest. Marching straight toward *hubris,*

hamartia, peripetia, those Greek cheers
we never learned, nor can I save them from.

I'm from Leominster: 48 Bonnydale Road,
address I'll die remembering. Couldn't

be prouder: 537–3581,
call anytime, from 1954–69.

Can't hear me now: leave a message on the machine.
I'll be coming back from time to time

when my pride's up. Yell a little louder:
Leominster, Leominster, Leominster!

at Delphi. Some judgment! Now I've got osteo-

necrosis, talk about the dead speaking through us.
The fountainhead cut off the flow to the corpus,

stanched the blood to the hip, specifically.
Now I'm limping with bum luck, arthritic, fully

dyscapable because—what?—I had the hubris
to guess a few answers to the oracle, such as

how *hubris* and *utterance* spring from the same root.
Since he's king of hysteron proteron, he sought

my fall and my coming before I came. At least,
he gave me no sign: Don't read to the tourists,

don't phoenix-like fly off the temple's north face,
reciting rhymed couplets of Alexandrine verse,

casting yourself as the falling caesura.
Perspective's deceiving as Delphic oracular:

a ten-foot drop is twenty, the Macedonian
cedars are plushy trees, not bushes; thus sane

men and women follow the signs and use the stairs.
For months I wore a cast, and the cast was dyed powder

blue from my smudged poems, my smug omphallic prophesies—
all wrong, as it turned out, years later, how hubris

too shares roots with *carouser, outsider, outlaw,*
all of which I became, in time, far from Apollo's

song and verse and medicine. Degenerative
arthritis has healed my wanderlust, the motive

for which his poultice stanched the original flow:
So you'd bleed poetry? Sit down, sir, and muse how

the sweetest nectar trickles from the caves of gods,
how the sacral place is silent, while youthful frauds

gush doggerel, fall ill, then slowly heal in time
to hear the merest trickle from the old sublime.

Oh, withered hips, I'm steadfast, staunch, seated in dark
interior rooms where poems wind among the rocks.

At last, I'm settled at my table, this small temple
from which words come, thinly, through my archaic smile.

FOUR

THE LANGUAGE

TREE

FRENCH LESSON

I had listened to classroom tapes
and Sorbonne-trained teachers
humiliate us in hundred-degree heat.
Constitutionally afraid of breezes, they kept
the windows closed, and we practiced the phrase
Il fait chaud until sweat dripped from our noses.
And all for the pleasure of love-worn phrases
breathed nasally: *J'taime.* To the woman
I loved more than *ma langue maternelle,*
I was willing to give up everything,
everything! *L'amour est aveugle.*

Finally, they cut us loose in the salt air—
our last exam on the deck of a fishing boat,
L'Esprit, with "authentic French fishermen"
slugging down morning brew and tearing
hard crusts of bread with their bright teeth.
As I retched over the gunnel, one oily
pecheur leered at my wife, motioning her
to snap his picture: *Je suis tres beau!*
He clutched the lanyard to secure the rigging,
hoisted the halyard and cranked the winch
for the trawling nets. (Ah, the language
a landlubber loses! I thought, clutching
the gunnel and retching.)

Then he bid us adieu,
flashing a lonely smile. Alone,
alongside his mates, he worked, untangling—
as the winch hauled them up—the kelp-encrusted nets,
two tons of silvery sardines and anchovies showering
down like writhing tongues, protesting the air
they could not breathe.

From that place
of fish offal, gurry and sord, his scarred, fastidious
hands sorted and scooped into boxes and crates
until the deck was picked seagull-clean, even a few broken
swordfish and skates boxed away – while I retched out
the mingled smells of engine exhaust, anchovies,
and the imminent departure of my wife
who would take her French fluency to the South Seas
while I went home to the old language of my poems,
to the old bed where one of two sagging
imprints would be missing.

From that distance
I would recall the captain's perch, how he tracked
with underwater radar the movements of fish,
scanned their oblong shapes for exactly what moved
under the surface. And I would track on a screen
lit with words the movements of my wife
through Polynesia, feel the language's inefficiency
as her constructions became more foreign,
and my own as well, as the roll and drift
of who we were, tied to how we say what we say,
grew queasy and amnesic, and how we each worked alone
to dredge for a language that would feed us,
the words writhing like tongues of flame
about to extinguish in the foreign air.

Snow deep in north pasture, more
On the way. How odd to read
Her letters, where light lies
Easy on Polynesian waves. She's
There on the quay or under the shade
Of mango and palm, draped in a red
Pareu, listening to the liquid
Sounds of their vowels.
Here, a month of zero
Mercury and words chuffed
In little clouds drifting off
To who knows where.
My brain's split between hemispheres.
Was there ever a year she desired
This house and pasture?
Don't lie. Of course, of course—
And yet—just yesterday
I broke through snowcrust
On a downward-sloping field,
Broke through to a deep-running
Spring we'd discovered years ago
When we built here. That gusher
Down in the foundation—we were
Astonished at the water's force.
Half-feared it would obliterate
Concrete, and half-desired it—
Our house balanced on a spume,
A great spinning, shining ride
In the revolving years
Of early love. It almost washed
The backhoe clean as it struck
The source. Later, the force
Lessened to a stream

Manageable and constant.
We diverted it with a simple
Lead pipe out to the field
And forgot about it.
Until now, until I broke through.
Snow falling on my blue parka,
Blue gloves, blue hat. I know
Where this stream ends—
Where all the springs drain—
Down at the bottom of the pasture
Where birches bend under all this
White weight, and swamp begins.
And nothing but willows grow
In the boggy hummocks, iced up now,
Their roots lifted up
As if trying to take a first, slow step
Out of the rime and ooze. And every living
Thing falls down into the watery spaces
They've abandoned.

Zero. Sunlight.
River's gurgle
muffled under ice.
Where do brook trout go?
How does ice become them?
Their brains slow to tableau
vivant. To know ice that close-
ly! Then thrash alive in spring.

On ice, I'm blind:
the sun's dazzling
performance, light with-
out heat, reflects a
surface diamond-sharp. Life's
unreflected, encased
in ice, or flowing under
ice floes. No mirror here shows

passion's answer.
At Hayden's shack,
only wordplay winks
at me, lovely light
in the capped and hooded
head. Sparkle. Parka. Home-
spun puns in the ice of i-
solation. Whatever words

alone can do,
they do. The heart's
another matter,
needing kindling, but
just now I'm out of luck.
My love life's frozen deep.

The old woodstove's no match for
this cold snap. My fingers freeze.

My hungers cease.
My arms encase
me, fused like wings. A
singing chickadee
flits tree to tree, bird-body
in league with cold *dee-dee*
of bird-mind. What does it know
of zero? It knows its body,

if not its mind,
will zip up limbs
looking for summer
bugs preserved like freeze-
dried peas. Jesus, where has
Hayden gone? How did he
outlast this cold, hold chaos,
snow, at bay. How? Why, love's

interventions:
warmth and wit, great
sense and sentiment
for dear Rose Marie,
dear *liebe*, who lives here
still, alone, still lively
in her age. She gave him his
voice, his cold peculiar

rage to chastise
others with love,
with *brothers, I loved*

you all. Bejesus,
he says now his mind is
moving toward zero, too.
Now his poems are frozen in
neural pools, each phrase encased

in musing ice,
unaware of
the silver sparkle,
flashing undersides,
one pool over—unless
sun in league with summer,
and love in league with matter,
melts the whole ice-dammed river!

Jesus, I'm heed-
less of zero's
estate. I'll study
how shadows—as sun
moves, heedless of us, cross-
ing our afternoon—grow.
Imagine them—Hayden, Rose—
shadows lengthening by sun's

command, now swoon
across snow, lie
long in blue day's un-
doing, and marry
eventual sunset.
Fire's out. My fingers,
still numb, now cradle a match,
ignite the oldest news, try

to grasp what drew
me to this shack
from the start: his poems
that love spawned, imag-
ining I could unfreeze
the passions from the man.
I can't. He's blocked in ice or
swimming too far down to seize.

Perilously close to closing the door
On the season of dolor and stupor.
Perilously close to lethargy's lease
Date. The contract's up, the buttercups
Will sashay in. Any day, now.
Any day. O what will become
Of winter covers, of slow recoveries
From colds, from cold lovers. Percolating
Whole days. Musing over hot soup. How
Easy to tuck under a comforter or ease
Down by the woodstove, conking at eight
Or nine. Daylight long gone. Bothering
Someone else with its knock and promise
On the southern curve of the world. Perilous
The awakening, the suicide bridge
Thawing for the March leap, the half-asleep
Ones fumbling with their blinds, blinking back
All they have not accomplished, blinking back
At the new slant of light, then leaping and
Aiming—*aiming*—for that black hole
In the ice that was yesterday coated
Over, silver and shining and wholly closed.

She's downstairs making trees.
Trees that grow downward
toward their noun clause

and verb clause. As if trees,
inverted, stripped leaf from
leaf, could still cohere.

It's how we make meaning,
she says. It's how we
clarify. Tonight,

let's plot transformations:
pronominal reclusions: *we*
into *you* and *I.*

Half-whispers in the cellar—*Chomsky,*
Chomsky—breeze through branches
of trees whose phrases,

like leaves, grow further
and further from the acorn-kernel
of meaning. Diagram that, please.

Diagram why we lost the forest
for the trees. And words, words,
words later she still couldn't say.

Chomsky, Chomsky. The sky's
the limit, where language comes
against a vacuum, an absence

of air for aspirants
of love's evasions. No lies
rise above seven miles.

Great comfort for astronauts, not,
I think, for earth-bound husbands,
clods like me, rooted

in what's unsaid. She's lost
the forest for the trees? Words
have common origins, she says.

They come from families. *Yes,
yes?* Sometimes they're torn,
she says, attached to two

competing word groups. *Yes,
yes?* So much depends upon
how one reads the attraction.

What's unsayable, unread, the underside
of the sentence, she'll diagram
by morning. I'll read it then.

PREDATORY MEN

There are predatory men, she says,
whose image is lean, forward-leaning, sharp-
mouthed hunger. If you're gentle, you're swallowed
whole. If you struggle, there's blood.
If there's a genetic code for them, it reads *smooth-
skinned, sleek, relentless*. Tireless cruisers,
they're magnetic up and down their lengths. Apparently,
she met such men and swam among them.
In the South Seas, natives called her
she who survives the sharks.
But they did not have to live
with the aftermath. Love's not a feeding
frenzy, nor endless in its hunger.
Stop for a moment the forward progress,
stop the hunt for talk's sake, stop to prod soft spots
beneath the tough skin, and watch the white teeth
open and close. What is weakness but words
shared across an empty space? Not these men.
You were either in their mouths, in their bellies,
cruising on high-blooded adventure, or you were nowhere.
Which is why she eventually washed up here,
scarred, starved for language. And I,
whose image is beefy, back-leaning, soft-
spoken, whose words fall often into past tense,
I paid attention to the pressure in my head
as I went down, down with her, as I listened
to the sighs and whispers of her long year,
body-sobs like the bends, painful utterances,
then concession, yes, that those others
are out there, circling and circling our homes.

I like road signs out of season,
and someone else's sweat
on my brow, the unexpected
taste of her last meal
in my mouth as I drive,
and the way she cleans up
when she's done. I like how she
points to the unexpected

lights of Breezewood
as the car spurts through Blue Mountain Tunnel,
shudders down Sidelong Hill
and languorous central Pennsylvania
opens around us.

Later, we sit in the evolving
restaurant, smell ghosts
of cigarettes on vinyl,
and trace black stains on the table
where a lit tip burned
too long over a pregnant
pause. We're trying,
believe me, to be responsible.

Trying to try. But the world's
not a cultivated pearl; more a sexual
irritant closed between the half shells
of our brain. Something could come
from any clammy embrace.

Which leads to Breezewood, ambivalence,
our arms stuck to the tabletop.
Do we want the little pearl

we've made, the white cell floating
on a computer screen like a pendant
on black velvet—that will,
if we say yes, string cell
to cell until the whole
genetic chain encircles us?

We're trying to imagine the weight
of a babe in our arms, the startle
of a crying mouth, the start of love
beyond us. Can we muster the courage,
the language, to get it up?

We've talked it to death, to the brink
of non-being. Where's the quirky
chemistry? Two gametes nose
to nose, Westward Ho! on a first journey.
Not like those hapless haploids
afraid to look in a mirror
and be somebody. Where are the fast kids
kidding each other with their turbo-

charged hot rods? Now they need
to put up or shut up. They need
to ride like big-rigs hauling California
fruit up Sidelong Hill, like ghosts of Conestogas
returning with their final freight of gold.

FIVE

BIRTH

ANNOUNCEMENTS

AMNIOCENTESIS

In ancient Greece, the *amnion*'s
a sacrificial plate to hold
a victim's blood. Four millennia

from that naming, I'm watching
a computer screen enlarge her
amniotic sac, the swirl of albumin

and pyin, the unfinished form
of our unnamed child. I'm watching
the hollow needle pierce the skin,

slide toward the womb, suck in
the solution that will tell us
the child's a healthy child.

If it's not, will it bear a name
or return to the greater anonymity,
victim of a bloody fate?

And what solution will wash
that speck of flesh and blood
from our hands? Four millennia

haven't cleansed us. The doctor
marshals the evidence, enlarges
the screen, reveals its watery home.

A white explosion
where the hollow needle strikes.
The foetus kicks and slaps

its uncompleted limbs.
This bright intrusion might be
a burning star, for all it knows,

a spent cinder hissing into the inner sea
from four millennia away.
There'll be no definite sighting.

Perhaps a memory of surprise.
A strange glimmer in the dark.
A first visit from another planet

where darkness alternates with light
and words abort their meanings
one generation at a time.

BIRTH ANNOUNCEMENTS

How could I have known, daughter,
the little cards that broadcast your birth

would feel so flimsy in my hands. No, it's not
the recycled paper, though there's a recycled

feeling. I plucked up these cards from the pharmacy,
right next to the ones wishing happy birthday,

long marriage, quick recovery, and our condolences.
Now I'm gazing out my window at a pasture

that no longer includes me, unable to move
into that bright past I lived in, oh, just an hour

ago, apple blossoms, summer's promised
winds, and now this: an all-too-human room

that sunset reflects back to me, a room
crowded with flowers and cards and you

centered in a cradle, and me somewhere at the edge
of the view, a man with Pampers in his hands.

Daughter, you for whom love goes, truly,
without saying, it's hard to be housebound,

housebroken. Though I dote on your coos
and saliva bubbles, your eyes of other-

worldly light, if you'd just open
a small window for me to come and go . . .

I know your moods blossom
for some other being. I watch and witness,

almost unmoved, as you practice
the glum line across your mouth,

the rounded pout, the cribbed smile.
As the sky darkens, your mood becomes mine,

little one, colic from an undiscovered country
passing through you like a ghost. Then I bump

against the window of your grief and see
a future so strange it hardly includes me,

landscapes of radiation and neon,
green grass still growing over tombstones.

You're leaning there over my bones and long,
long hair, trying to remember, to forget

how the sun is a blazing clock
that blinds us if we scrutinize its face.

I'm deep into my darkness, succumbed
to numbing cold—until the sun comes up.

Lazarus could not have tried harder than I will,
darling, to burst from that dark room

back into this one, this brightness
I'm still living in, watching neon red

cardinals pull green worms from the leaves,
and swallow them down. I'm comparing

occupations, little bud, preparing
to pluck up death, digest it, and still

fly into the punishing sun-struck world.

Anna's face turns upstream
toward the source, feeding
from Kate's breast. I'm faced
that way, too, sitting beside them
in the half-dark at half-past
something. Faced toward Creation's
good profile, if it has one.
And I'm feeding, too, off the night-
light's inventions: baby rattles
turn to swans on the ceiling,
crib bars become angelfish
on the walls. Other nights,
I've turned away to eye
baby mobiles dangling above me
like lures from the past, brazen
faces, garters scattered by a bed, unadult-
erated play. Gone in time's
wayward stream. Almost
retrievable. What turns me back
toward Anna's face is the fullest
nourishment. Her moon-face
floating under a swelled breast,
and Kate's face drifting above
her girl-child's. I imagine my own
wavering beside them on the couch,
turned toward whatever issues
out of nothingness, whatever grows
toward this feeding at this dim hour,
when sustenance seems far off,
or close at hand, flowing
down the current to me
if I will only open my mouth
and let the moment stream in.

Lawns lush and combed by oceanwind,
yachts and ferries gliding by on surfaces
of beaten silver. Lying here near lap-
ping waves, lull of privilege, we can't

relax. Braced against the earth, Kate lifts
our daughter skyward. Little Anna, up-
raised in her mother's hands, airborne
in a sky of laughing gulls, hawks circling

on thermals. What will she remember? Airy
abandon? Two columnar arms remote
as statues? Or something keener, seen from hawk's
hieratic eye? Daughter, how we have loved

the little square of sunlight that includes
you. A blanket, a patch of grass, altar
of our affections. The little neck that
wobbles and cannot hold its head aloft

holds our gaze and praises. How long can we lie
in the shade of lawn ornaments—black
lantern boys—saluting the upraised,
triangular glasses of yachters passing,

gliding between the jeweled islands
of Penobscot Bay. At ebbtide, mudflats
separate one perfect island
from another. Their granite sides

seem to breach in the bay like whales, sparkling
a moment in late sunlight, remote
yet tantalizingly close. Further off,
sunset's fairweather promise. Composed so,

possessed of calm minds, filled with the cadences
of drowsy cowbells and windchimes, almost stopped
by leisure's pace, what more could we want? Utter stillness. And still,
everything in motion. This scene, and the next

high tide where those in sputtering, pitted
fishing boats come home, those in the ferry's
aft decks move forward, and those who missed it
finally clutch a rail and make passage. This scene

and the next high tide where the perfect
islands coalesce in a lesser order.

I've left you, my daughter, for the first time,
quite cavalierly, to arrive at this colony.

And everything was planned, the wild, reclusive, looping lines
of mind's indulgence, the world's static filtered out.

But I had not reckoned with the twined song in my chest,
the subtle couplets you've written everywhere on my being.

I cannot hear my own voice without hearing yours. How odd,
this lyrical interference comes from another source,

another powerful voice whose self-promotions send waves
of song into the future. Shall I tune you out, set frequency

to something further down the dial, some golden oldies?
You're merely three years old, in love with this new language

that beams forth with every breath. You're all experiment:
Why is a madhouse a house that's mad? Where's the arrow

fired from the string of a rainbow? Little literalist, maker
of new meanings, the world's freshly sung, the forms undiscovered.

The waveband's broad enough to hum in four-dimensional time,
beyond AM, FM, shortwave, curving to the edge of time-

lessness where memory converts to song. Does love for what's gone
explode in sonic booms? Out there, in uncircumscribed air,

is the world circular? Can your eccentric namings bring me round
again, or will it all be squared by schoolmarms and golems?

Courage, little one, and songs of your own transmission.
Should you see me out there, along the edge, cosmic dust

in your eye, as my father was stardust for me, hum a few bars
of something unforgettable—as another singer

did for her father. Make it in quaint couplets across the
distances, and let these old emissions echo back to you.

Golden, Cortland, Empire,
McIntosh, Delicious,
even crab—in short,
she'll grab them all, my small
girl-child, in or out of season—
clutch summer's hard greens
or cradle fall's red survivors,
wormholes and all, she'll call them
her windfall, her doctor-a-day.
I'll call them her healthy
curiosities, her tongue's delight.
No wonder she wonders at their maker:
who cast the first seeds out
with a generous hand,
who colored the blossoms
white, then tinted their insides pink?
No wonder she's grown curious
and quick, sexual and rebel,
until she preempts all commands
from her father and orders him about:
that one, that one, no, that one!
In short, she's defenseless
against wonder, against inquisition's
pitfalls, that is, the Fall
into the Pit. Defenseless against apples
laced with law, or poison, or worm's
rotten intention. In short, her four
earth years have not prepared her
for clay's desire, air's shimmer,
water's oscillation, fire's agitation.
In short, she's sinking
her teeth into the green world.

DEER SEASON

My two-year-old hits the remote—
PAUSE—just as snow begins
to scumble Bambi and his mom
who wander toward the hunter's
scope—and the screen freezes.

She's never seen it, the mother's death,
but knows it's there, camouflaged in winter,
knows Bambi won't die with his mother,
will go on orphaned into the blood-
bright world, will mate, and father,

and stand guard, and hear at last
the inexorable cry of scavenging
birds that presage hunters everywhere.
We've told our daughter this much,
and so prepared her for the big outdoors,

the air alive with buckshot and bucks
shot. We walk the Cemetery Plot
Road, once a deer path, now a track
to deer camps. *Is that the sound—*
she asks—*the sound that makes me stop*

the video? Yes, that's the sound.
How does the bullet feel?
A question we can't answer
unless we live inside another skin.
The head explodes in these

questionings, star-burst, stag-
ger and fall into the world,
where eye's aqueous humor

dulls to a glassy lens,
the rack's hacked off, and mounted,

mounted for nothing, for pride, the body eaten,
by which they shall know uneternal
life. Pass the bluebottle around, a buzz
in their heads until they go
stone-cold in the Sportsman's Bar.

My morning prayer has both palms raised
above the keys, and now I strike
a word, strike it out, start again,
and slowly sight my way. May hers
be aerial vision, preferring
the earth's blue-green topography
to sun's white citadels. May she
light down each evening. My fingers
play the little chapel game with her,
point skyward, then home to the human
multitude bowed down in prayer.
I've never flown in dreams or spirit-
quests, in sky that wasn't sky. Earth-
bound, I've felt the weight of that sentence.
I look my talents in the eye
and claim them full of gravity.
May hers be buoyant, sparkling
in wit and spirit. May she lift
off early and stay aloft,
as she desires. Let the heart,
set in dust and clay, weigh what it
weighs. Let her hear, in my absence,
this psalm, whose singer, at last, will move
off the mud flats, toward open water.
May she read me as I read her,
from the other side of light.
May her readers accede to worlds
more dazzling than they could conceive.
May they be happy, and many.

(Vinalhaven, Maine)

How much of me is bound
to this hazy domestic morning, Kate's breasts
pressed against my back, her arms claiming
my middle, as we clear a circle of steam
from the bathroom mirror and discover
Anna's baby face with ours, a trinity
of smiles above the rippling tub.
And how much of me startles
with the foghorn's warning
into the morning calisthenics
of separation.

I arise and go
to my writing room, Kate to the morning's
nursing, the drowsy, milky hours ahead.
Later, they'll awake to the day: off with the sleep
suit, the diaper, the nightly excretions; on with the diaper,
the summer-jumper, the morning explorations. Tomorrow
it's my turn. Waves of duty wash in, wash out.

I've been reading the local lore:
sea monsters shadow the harbors, born of anything
we cast off. Shape-shifters, they return
to us the negative space
of our obsessions. Yesterday,
a yachting family in the bay—
the kids' watery horseplay, the parents' mid-day
cocktails—and suddenly I saw a serpent's silvery back
rise from the sea, devour the ship, and disappear.
Again and again, held to the same spot,
until a cloud occluded the sun
and I understood how their polished hull
diverted brightness into silver scales
rising from the water to dazzle my eyes.

If the yacht's still there today,
my mind skims past it, further out,
where humid Gulf Stream bumps up against the frigid Labrador,
and fogs are born full-grown, their appetites
enormous, ready to swallow their sea-parents,
if need be, ready to rear up and close over the rim
of the world.

Now, Anna caterwauls,
colic passing through her like ghosts
from an undiscovered country. She wails
until the whole cottage fills with her troubles,
washes over each private room. Sleep-deprived, fogged in,
the whole mental house is underwater . . .

Out there, where two currents become one,
where bonita and redfish merge with cod and haddock,
where warm infusions of plankton meet the green ice of glaciers,
I still hear the foghorn's moan of separation, hear it now
touching every lost boat, every misguided spirit at the edge
of the fogbank where light dissolves and gives nothing back . . .

A brief window opens in the fog—
the shore sedge swims into view,
primrose and Queen Anne's lace, a vague
shadow of roof and chimney nearby.
Kate and Anna are out walking the harbor
road, the house quiet.

Now fog closes in again, hedges
the yard's interior, covers the community
of mosses and blueberries and granite ledges.
And now it encloses the house: even the flag

with its fifty stars of union hanging off
our deck is eclipsed; even the colorful
symmetry of flowers in the flower box
dissolves. Tires screech on the harbor
road. Kate and Anna shrouded.
I fish for my keys in the fog
of the living room, barely find my way
to the end of this sentence to go out.

SIX

TRUSTING THE LAND'S PURE CURVE

Here, another season of mellow fruitfulness.
Bees drowsing in fallen apples, maple leaves
leading where they've always led: downward
to stubble fields.

One county over, in the exploding
suburbs, dirt roads are smothered—
the oily scam of macadam—and
pastures bulldozed of their bulls.

Listen. Listen hard. You'll hear it:
the *beep-beep-beep* of something backing up—
backhoe, dump truck—sweeping up what's past,
then moving forward, closer to our future.

Let's break the law and put a billboard
on the county line. Let some old nature
goddess gaze out on the two-lane and speak
a mouthful to the passing motorists:

New mansions of Jericho,
let your walls tumble down.
New malls of Saint Albans,
let the season's sweet decay

jog shoppers from their purchases
as they whirl past on their way
to checkout counters. Measure progress
by what trees give back to the forest floor.

Measure it by pastures mown of their excess.
The blades will lie down easily, revive
without past lives of grass crowns
to slough off.

TRUSTING THE LAND'S PURE CURVE *(for Roger Peterson)*

There is seldom more than a man
to a harrowed piece.
—Robert Frost

1

    how after walking through chokecherry blossom
you come to a mossed stone wall. Where there's a gap
in stones you think "gate and cobbled roadway,"
and take it back further into forest.

Losing the road in dusk, you pocket compass
and survey map, go by the land's pure curve—
back between those younger trees where pasture
was carved, stumps plowed under, and one
small-farmer lived after his own way.

Further on, you read another dozen
stories of the faded farms until you come
to their Vermont town and rest on the rusted
seat of a Model T, smell the rotting
barnboard of a general store, and dream
of the Yankees who walked these hard-packed streets.

    how following the road back, you know
there is no road but the one you've made
on a topographic map, your pencil's
broken dashes across the elevation
lines tracing the mind's bond to the land.

2

Years later, you climb to the place
where a culvert diverts a rushing stream

and learn the calculus by which men
abandon the uncontrollable seasons
of wind and rain. Bodies still vanish

in flashfloods, boulders click like marbles
over sleeping villages. One equation
will build a dam in a river of whitewater
and cast a safe shadow over the towns.
Now you imagine rounding a mountain
turn, to come upon, at dusk, industrious
towns—your way lit wholly with water.

All day these visions glint behind your eyes.
Immersed in the hum of machines, you wander
far from your body and hardly notice
the light dimming to autumn, the leaves
flickering and going out, the trail cold.

3

The snowshoe rabbits you stalked and caught
huddle in their hutch, perhaps breed safely,
and all their brethren survive. Perhaps
remember the small hungers in winter air,
the thorn in the fur where the hare shivers

in its thicket. Today you regret
the scars have faded where blackberry bushes
once scratched your face. There's little trace of the wild
blood on your lips. Dead leaves have fallen

over the old roads: stone gaps open wide
inside you. Would you walk back now into your life,
trusting the land's pure curve for direction?

4

Or would your well-trained eyes peruse the lines
of survey maps, conclude the fallen stones
were nothing but the natural fault lines
of the aging world, and turn, and return
home the well-marked way you first had come?

Or would you, as I want you, read those gaps
as stories seeking your return, to take back
further into forest where the voice is
not your own but now the property

of one who lived after his own way,
sleeping easily beside the tumbled
general store where pine and birch thrust
tangled limbs out through the roof and windows.

ON THE OCCASION OF PAUL CARRIERE'S DEATH

(Thanksgiving Day, 1995)

Inarticulate now as he who disappeared
under the iron back of his tractor.
Hauling logs on a steep Vermont slope,
he rolled under the hard mechanism
of his life's work and lay pinned
by the wheel. I'm making it up
as I go—no neighbor to relay the details—
and without them he's leaving the earth
too soon: firefighters have already levered
the tons of steel from his chest, the ambulance
has already plucked him from November
leaves and mud, car have carried mourners
to his widow's home beneath the hundred-year cottonwoods,
the adze-planed edges of the closed casket
have been prepared, and the realtor
come with his hammer and sign.

There has been no time
to fit myself into the proceedings, I who knew him
passably enough to know the depth of our differences
and still to admire the burly, barrel-chested farmer
who brush-hogged my fields and rehearsed the history
of this hilltop. To stand with him and survey
the acres before he mowed them was to prepare
each time for his death. To stand, spit, and talk
across the distances of our chosen lives—
the farmer and the teacher—to hear
in our exchanges the cringing clichés
of two men lost to each other—to hear
yet more than this, some tentative figure
groping along the stonewall of two men's
mental properties and arriving finally at the gap
where the old carriage road once thrived

with farmers, teachers, and all the odd
figures of the community, and take it back
to the 1940s when Paul Carriere farmed alone
on this hillside, fashioned a rope-tow
during mudseason to skim his milk jugs
down to the village. And back further
to the first plot owners of the 1840s
who planted cottonwoods, raised the house,
trees and house growing together, the house
doubling, doubling again as generations
of farmers milked, hayed, froze, and endured.

        Until Paul bought the farm in '45,
farmed, froze, fell, and rose up again, time
after time, herd after herd, until time passed him by
for good at the swishing tail-end of the century,
and he joined the farming legions going under.
Then rose again and turned his hand to even smaller-
scale miracles of survival, carpentry, logging,
fieldwork, and talking, delivering our firewood,
hammering our homes, rehearsing, reharrowing
the local hilltop history . . . until this Thanksgiving
when the iron machine reared up and crushed him,
and his moment of going

        is upon us, where I've tried to hold him
before he vanishes into history, into the hillside
cemetery beneath the chiseled stones, or crosses
the sidereal isthmus, the blueblack azimuth
to the place I've always imagined beyond imagining,
where he can perch on the crown of those hundred-year
cottonwoods, sing for all he was worth,
and I can let him go.

EVERY MORNING

Garbage men idle in their garbage
truck in a pull-off spot with a dawn
view. I'm up with them watching
their sweet waste waft up and bring down
the crows, who call and circle as if
over a dying beast. I'm trying
to guess their aesthetic, silly
as it sounds, wherever the sweet
spot in their bodies is, the leisure
that causes them to stop here.
Is it the mountain view, the mown pasture,
or just a place to flick butts
from the cab and ogle at the jogger
on her dawn run, the slim retiree
whose manse nearby in what used to be
south pasture is covered now in flowers.
And what's her highest pleasure?
She's at it every morning by six,
turning the compost pit, manuring
the beds, bending and straightening
her back, out there every morning
in her bikini top and running shorts,
leathery, gray-haired, lively.
Days ago, I startled the guy
who parks his pickup here beside
north pasture every morning—
after the garbagemen go—
enjoying, I imagine, the morning
his way, windows down, smoking,
reading the news, smoking, taking in
the view, then back to news.
Lately, he'd turned up his radio,
country music jangling and twangling

over the hay. I knocked on his cab
and told him straight: I don't like sound-
tracks with my nature, the birds
dubbed out, the wind a syncopation
between notes of a hillbilly bass line.
Well, the guy startled—he was young
and dark—deeply tanned, black shock
of hair, well-muscled, and violent
in his face, his gruff "Excuse me
for livin'!" before he choked
the ignition, stomped the gas, and spun
his tires in a spray of gravel and dust.
I felt bad but I felt right, too.
I wasn't denying him his view
but was limiting his pleasure,
the old compromise between one nature
and another, between a human song
and the wind's. Now he's on my mind
again. I wrote down his license plate—
just in case—some endangered bird
preceding the identifying numbers
that showed, I guess, he was more than
the gun rack on the back of his cab
and for everything he shot
there was something he gave back.
Now he's gone and put a hole in this
early morning as yesterday
his father found him dead, down there
in what we call the Johnson slum, a self-
inflicted gun wound to the head.
I didn't know him but for the picture
in the morning papers. He lived
and died in a dark apartment

shaded by a fire escape, but he liked
the open air, his father told the local
news, he liked every morning
rising early, to take the morning air.

1

There's a green horse,
a miniature, coated
in circles of glitter,
a sort of armor
over armature
by which the hollow
horse hangs together, hangs
from the candelabra

above my head.
Beyond's the window
and further on, more green
galloping across spring
lawn, green leaves of choke-
cherry, raspberry, green blades
beside the brook bleeding
it green. May is

brilliant to the point
of vanishing. Remove
one sun-struck thing,
blacken it with night-
frost or voracious air's
blights and spores:
the thing goes slack
or colorless or rust,

caves in to the shaded
world of this writing shack
where the wiring's blown,
candles lit above green
horse's mane in

broad daylight, super-
fluous and serious,
yellow cautions.

2

Old eyes squint from May
light but remember what
it means: bright pulse
of forever in the blood.
Oh, take it, young ones.
lovers, take it in loins
and bones. Take it inside
for the little time

it's yours. I'm past tenses.
I'm future unfolded, plot
complete. How awful to be
known. I can't look on it:
green against blue's flawless
sky, brook water running fast—
blue-green in its veins—
over gray stones. Green

rushes on. And old stones,
speckled in spring light—
green half-moons or scythes
rippling above them, by which
it seems they too move—
remain at bottom gray
and cold, as always.
Were they ever moved

at all along the riverbed?
Were they washed and rolled,
chipped and changed in spring's
green? Were they nothing
but gray armature
beneath green water,
gray keepsakes
in place, all this time.

Feeling possessive, sitting at Hayden's
old writing table? Study the never-
repeating snowflakes. There's a lot of air
out there, unused, unmarked, a storm
of self-revealing that reads too late
its own drift and dispersal. You're heir
to nothing. And nothing's heir to you.
Scratch and watch your skin flake off
to join the greater swirl of snow,

a morning marked and forgotten in a storm-
visited life, as all lives are so visited—
one out of the many, one out of history's
minions, with as much snow blowing
in an inner sky, as many days lost
to whiteouts, as many drifts obscuring
the footsteps one was following,
as well as one's own footsteps.
All of it forgotten as this air,

this day will be forgotten, drifting on,
washing clean the sky's gray slate . . .
Oh yes, marked, briefly, by the latest
occupant to scratch his X on this house
of moving air, scattering his being—
a few sparse flakes—that try, and fail,
to connect the dots of some wished-for
larger presence, whose name and residence,
as always, is unknown.

for Hayden Carruth

thought at muscled twenty. Now your body's
soft, growing moss, and so becoming
part of history, too, like that stunning
monostone across the stream you saw just now
and crossed over and found yourself reduced
by that enormous cliff broken
from some higher place. Perspective shifts
when you're a smaller piece
of the planet. Let the eye travel upward
toward that hilltop flat and peaceful with pines,
and know from some higher precipice once
a piece of rock broke off
and landslid down to this brook's babble
and lodged here until time without chronicler
lapped its sides to shiny skipping pebbles
and what piece was left on shore, a piece
large as a museum, began to house its artifacts
of fox and bear, for their tracks
are still here, and hosted crowds of lichen
and moss upon its roof that broke down
like mortar to pestle the rock to soil and now
a Christian era later hemlock and fir
stand straight and silent as museum guards.
Ask them why this green shade draws the eye
toward its deepest declivities.
Ask them where exactly this trickling stream
issues from, from what higher place the first
rains gathered and carved their rushing course.
Ask in vain how you're part of it,
without name or date, and why this brook will shush
us up who try to ask too much, will lap
instead at our feet and hands, saying skip
this stone across the stream or skip yourself
to the other side.

THE WEATHER WORD IS

Pelting rain out of the east,
Gulf storm come up the coast,
then blowing overland over cold
mountains. Weather's never local,
nor predictable. Cast a cold
eye on it and it's hail—
freezing in the heavens—
or sleet—freezing on earth—
in either case, hard weather-words,
Old English, that fell on their heads,
as on ours. It comes from the east,
from across the migrant seas,
from nearly twenty centuries
away. *Slete. Hagol. Freas.*
Those old transitional forms
between men who pronounced endings
and those now who don't. Who firm
their syllables—"a gathering
of letters"—like closed fists.
Cast a cold eye on this shift
of forms, betwixt one heaven's
haymakers and another's, words
that remind us we've grown hard—
sleet, hail, freeze—and hard weather's
met with lips set, a firm *God damn.*
But the old forms say it's as cold
down here as up there, given
certain inclemencies,
and a sun bearing what it bears—
from above, to below—makes a world
of difference, makes a world
that hail froze over, unfreeze.

Despise the mosquito's
precision, its slow injection

and withdrawal. A pinprick
on the skin. We're black fury. Flesh-

fevered. Our signature's
the rose bruise. The raised welt. Slapdash

to drink in the vein's blue
rivers, immerse and rise in red.

We're gyrating shimmers
jabbing the corners of your eyes.

Do we terrify? Think
Paolo and Francesca. We're love

bites on the jawline,
behind the ear, under the knee,

back of the thigh, hidden
caresses. As Orpheus sought

Eurydice, so we
journey down, down into the skin,

into veins requiring
life's sharp oxygen to turn jewel-

red again. Who are you,
bolted behind screens, itching welts

in the shade? Fall in love
with your wounds. Follow us into

the sun, and embrace, yes,
life's bloody feast, these open wings,

the sultry fury
inside whatever really lives.

ACKNOWLEDGMENTS

Poems in this manuscript appear or are forthcoming in the following magazines: *American Voice:* "From the Bridge at Taos"; *Boulevard:* "Teenager: 13"; *Chautauqua Literary Review:* "Hunger" and "The Immortal"; *Crab Orchard Review:* "Sunflower Sutra" and "Oh, on an April Morning"; *Harpur Palate:* "Duets"; *Hunger Mountain:* "Leap Day"; *The Journal:* "On the Occasion of Paul Carriere's Death"; *Many Mountains Moving:* "Amniocentesis"; *Meridian:* "Black Fly" and "Memento Mori"; *New England Review:* "Corfu"; *North American Review:* "Teenager: 19"; *Notre Dame Review:* "Romanticism in Virginia" and "The Weather Word Is"; *Ontario Review:* "Anna's Apples" and "Deer Season"; *Paris Review:* "Youthful, I Fell off the Temple of Apollo"; *Ploughshares:* "Waterfall at Journey's End"; *Rivendell:* "Every Morning"; *Saranac Review:* "Birth Announcements"; *Third Coast:* "Sick Day" and "Bridge Freezes before Road"; *Triquarterly:* "Hayden's Writer's Shack's Latest Occupant"; *The Blueline Anthology* (Rick Henry, Editor, Syracuse University Press): "Afternoon Sun, Zero Degrees"; *Contemporary Poets of New England* (Robert Pack and Jay Parini, Editors, University Press of New England): "Trusting the Land's Pure Curve" and "Autumn Progress: Rural Vermont"; *Verse Daily* (on-line journal reprinting poems from print journals): "Oh, on an April Morning."